TECOLOTE

ALSO BY SANDY NATHAN

Stepping Off the Edge: Learning & Living Spiritual Practice

Numenon (Bloodsong Series I)

The Angel & the Brown-eyed Boy (Tales from Earth's End I)

TECOLOTE

THE LITTLE HORSE THAT COULD

SANDY NATHAN

VILASA PRESS

SANTA YNEZ, CALIFORNIA

ISBN-13:   978-0-9762809-9-6
ISBN-10:   0-9762809-9-X
Library of Congress Control Number: 2010930451

Editor: Kathryn Agrell
Cover and interior design: Lewis Agrell
Photo credits: Zoe Nathan, cover photo

First Printing: 2011
Printed in the United States of America

            Publisher's Cataloging-in-Publication Data

Nathan, Sandra Oddstad.
   Tecolote : the little horse that could / Sandy Nathan.
      p. cm.
   ISBN: 978-0-9762809-9-6
   1. Horses—Juvenile literature. 2. Paso fino horse. (Peruvian Paso horse.) 3. Ranch life—Juvenile literature.   I.
Title.
SF302 .N37 2010
636.1—dc22
                                    2010930451

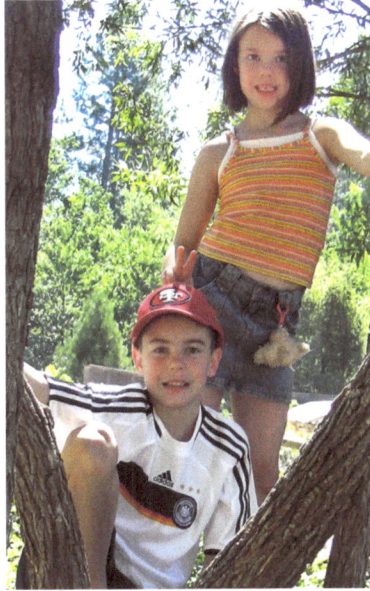

To my grandchildren Cara and Jarrett
and to grandchildren of all ages

A Surprise

"We'd better call Dad," Lily said, "just to make sure everything's all right." My daughter Lily and I were headed for a gospel concert. We were already in the spirit, clapping and laughing as we drove through the twilight in our lovely valley.

I pulled out my cellphone and dialed home. Things weren't all right—I could tell the instant I heard Barry's voice.

"I need you," he said. "Rosie had her baby. He's early. He can't stand up. I need help."

"We'll be right there." We whipped the car around, all thoughts gospel and joy gone.

We had bred horses for almost twenty years. We knew that baby horses need all the time they can get inside their mothers. A baby horse that's born just two weeks early probably won't make it. His little lungs may not be able to give him the air that he needs. He'll be too weak to stand or nurse.

Rosie's baby was ten days early. He could die.

The little horse came so fast that Barry didn't have time to catch Rosie and put her in a warm stall. She was in the pasture where she'd lived with Avispa, another mare who was expecting a baby. (Avispa's name means "bumblebee" in Spanish.) The mares were best friends.

Avispa had never seen a baby horse. She was curious and excited. She wanted to take a look. Avispa moved closer to the new baby, her ears pricked forward. She nickered to the foal.

"Who are you? What's your name?" she said in horse talk.

The closer Avispa got to the baby, the angrier Rosie became. She ran at Avispa and then dashed back to her baby. She did it again and again. Rosie was so angry at the other horse that she almost stepped on her foal. She thought her friend was going to hurt her little one, but she was the danger.

"Help me, Lily! Let's get Avispa out of here," Barry shouted. The two of them caught Avispa and put her somewhere safe, where Rosie couldn't see her.

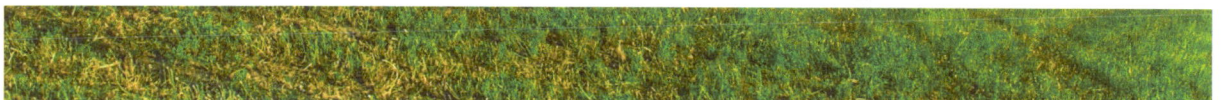

Avispa wanted to see the baby.

We turned to the new mama and the tiny shape laying in the grass.

The foal moved, but just barely. He couldn't stand; he could hardly raise his head. He was a pale beige little thing with a black mane and tail. A buckskin. We could see that he was a beauty, even lying down in the almost dark.

Rosie and Barry had been friends for years. Not anymore! Rosie pinned her ears back and charged him. Her teeth snapped. She spun around to kick.

Barry jumped away. Rosie wouldn't let him close. The more he tried to help the baby stand, the more upset she got. She didn't watch for her baby, and she didn't notice where she put her hooves.

Chasing Barry, she accidentally stepped on her foal. She didn't step on him enough to hurt him, but it was hard enough that we knew Rosie might kill her baby if we stayed.

Lily and I left the field and stood outside watching. Rosie guarded her foal, pacing restlessly, looking as though she'd try to kill us if we came in again.

It was a cold day, more like winter than spring.

The pasture was a green meadow studded with oak trees whose trunks were wider than my arms could reach. They arched high overhead, home to birds and squirrels. The meadow was a beautiful home for two fine mares, but it was so cold that night. The wind shook the trees, and we buttoned our coats.

It was May. Why was it so cold? Southern California isn't cold in May. Our breath formed puffs in front of us. We could see it in the evening light.

Barry stood near Rosie. The baby horse lay on his side, raising his head from time to time, trying to pull himself on to his tummy so he could try to stand up. He couldn't.

We knew how bad things were from our years of raising other horses. The baby needed to stand and drink his mother's milk. Human children have shots to protect them from getting sick, but baby horses get their protection from their mother's first milk. That milk gives them what they need to stay well until they're big enough to have shots like children and bigger horses do.

If a baby horse doesn't get that first milk, it can get very sick. Rosie stood glaring at us. She put back her ears and showed us her teeth. She turned and lifted her back feet as though she was going to kick us.

How was the baby going to get the milk he needed? How was he going to stand up? How was he going to live through the cold night? It was supposed to get down to thirty degrees that night—that's *freezing*.

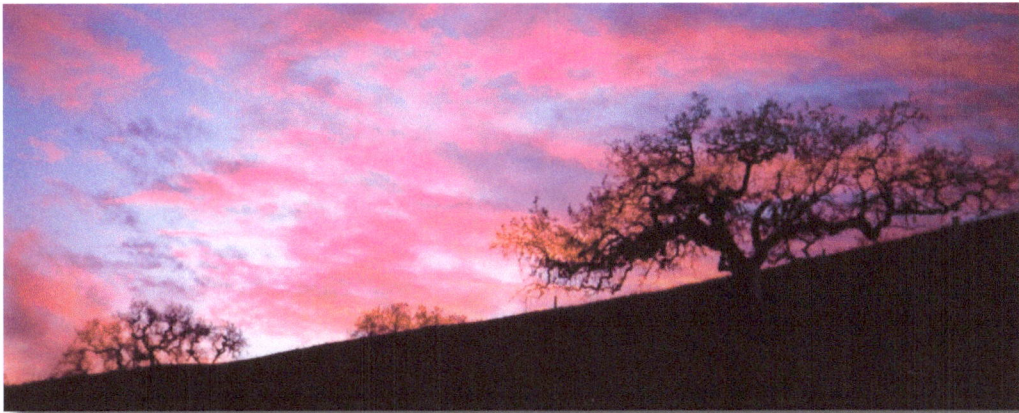

It was cold and dark and the baby horse couldn't stand

We called the veterinarian—the horse doctor. He said to put Rosie and her baby in the barn. But how could we?

Barry tried to catch Rosie one more time. She bit him so hard that it made a terrible bruise on his arm. Lily and I heard her teeth click together. We couldn't go near her or her baby.

Even if Barry could catch Rosie, we'd still be in trouble. Lily would have to lead Rosie to

the stable so he could carry the baby horse. The baby was early, but he still weighed so much that Lily and I could not lift him.

Lily *couldn't* handle Rosie. She was wild and dangerous, snapping and charging. We couldn't put her in a warm stall.

We were all alone in the dark with no one to help us. And it was getting colder.

What should we do?

We called the vet again. He said, "The foal will be okay. Baby horses have made it even in the snow. I'll be there in the morning."

So we went to bed, but we could hardly sleep. Barry's arm was black and blue and swollen where Rosie bit him. We were sure the baby would freeze.

As soon as the sun came up, I ran to the pasture.

A New Day

The baby was alive! But he was so weak he could barely raise his head. I cried and Lily cried. But—it was a new day!

Tony was there. Tony is our helper. He is a wonderful man. He fixes our garden and anything that's wrong in our house. Mostly, Tony trains our horses!

Tony works magic with horses. He's kind and gentle, and he can get horses to do anything.

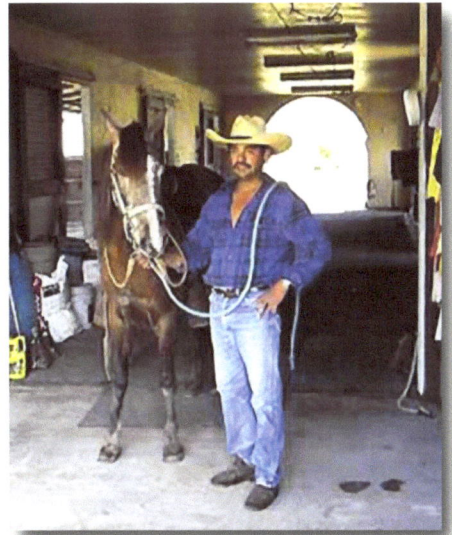

Tony and Barry caught Rosie. She wasn't crazy with Tony. He calmed her down. Barry led Rosie to a small, safe corral and Tony carried the new baby behind her. They put soft straw in the corral to make a bed and waited for the vet to come.

A good man

Did you know that brand new baby horses have their own special doctors to take care of them, just like human babies do? A special doctor for baby horses came from our veterinarian's hospital.

She put bandages on the little guy's front legs so they'd stay straight so he could stand up. She listened to his heart and looked into his eyes.

She said, "If he makes it for five days, he'll be okay."

Those were five long days. Lily and I sat next to the corral and prayed for the baby. Everyone in the neighborhood came by to see the colt and wish him well. They stood by the fence and watched and prayed. Many of them cried.

We named him *Tecolote*, which means "owl" in Spanish. You say Tecolote like this: Táyco-low-tay. We called him Tecolote because he was brown and black like an owl. He had big owl eyes. We called him Teco (Táy-co) for short.

He is a Peruvian Paso horse. Long ago, the Spanish brought horses like him to a country called Peru in South America. Peruvian Paso horses are very smooth to ride. They are given Spanish names or names from Indian words.

At one point, Teco looked pretty bad. His ribs went in and out so fast as his lungs tried to give him air. He didn't move. He was just too little to be out in the world.

I started to cry and said, "Take him to the hospital! Take him to the hospital right now!"

Barry didn't think it was a good idea, and I got mad at him. Do you ever get upset with people you love when you're afraid? I was afraid.

The vet was there. She said, "He can't be with his mom in the hospital. She'll get upset. And so will he. Why don't we wait a while?"

That was the smart thing to do because …

Tecolote got better. And guess what? Because he had so many people handling him when he was a tiny baby, he loved people. He was such a friendly little horse!

Tecolote lived in the little corral with his mother for two weeks, getting stronger.

Rosie and Tecolote in their corral

Tecolote was just fine!

In those weeks, he learned many things. He learned to lie down and stand up. Baby horses have very long legs and they wobble all over. He had a hard time getting up. If he got up, he didn't know how to get down. But he kept trying.

Lily and I watched him and laughed. He fell over trying to get up. He took a step and wobbled.

Tecolote learned to lie down.

He fell down. Everyone laughed. The neighbors came by and laughed instead of crying.

And he learned! Then he hopped and played and ran all over his little corral. What a funny baby horse!

A New Friend

While Tecolote and Rosie were in their little nest and Teco was getting stronger, something wonderful happened. The other mare, Avispa, had her baby.

We named him *Shambho*, which means "he who causes great joy in my heart." That name fits him. He was not born too early, and he was very strong. The picture was taken when he wasn't even a day old. See how he runs next to his mother? Most baby horses can get up and run soon after being born.

Avispa and her baby, Shambho

When Teco was two weeks old, we put him and Rosie in the green pasture with Avispa and her baby. Rosie had forgotten

how angry she was at Avispa that cold night. The mares were best friends again. The two mares and their babies had plenty of room to run and play.

Baby horses play just like puppies and kitties. They run and wrestle and pretend to fight. They chase each other.

Tecolote and Shambho sniffed noses when they met. Tecolote is buckskin; Shambho is palomino.

Avispa played with them, even though she was a grown-up horse.

This is how baby horses play:

Shambho would go up to
Tecolote and say, "I am
going to bite you."

Teco would say, "I'll
bite you back!" Then
they'd chase each other.

The two mares and babies had a wonderful time together. The colts grew and grew.

Rosie and Teco loved each other very much.

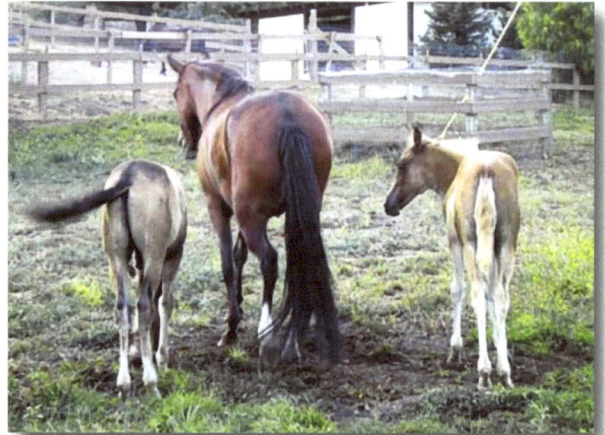

Some days, they just hung out together.

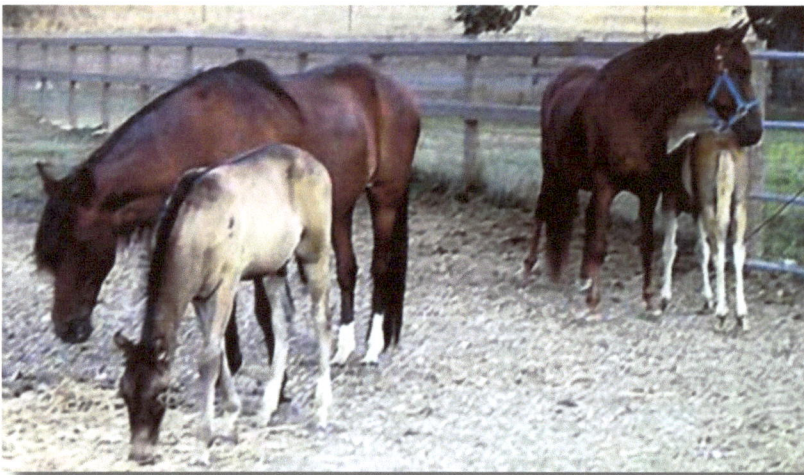

Rosie and Teco, and Avispa and Shambho: Mommies and babies growing and loving each other.

One thing about life: No matter how good things are or how bad, everything changes. Nothing lasts forever.

A Sad Day

One day, when Teco was five months old, something very sad happened. Rosie was old and had been sick for years—that's why she had Teco earlier than she was supposed to.

While he grew up and became bigger and stronger, Rosie became weaker and weaker. She could hardly walk. She took care of Teco until he didn't need her anymore.

And then she died.

We cried so much. Rosie was a good, dear friend. We had her since she was a young horse.

Lily cried the most: Rosie was Lily's special horse. She loved her just like she was another person. They had many great times.

When Lily used to show horses, she won many prizes on Rosie.

A dark day

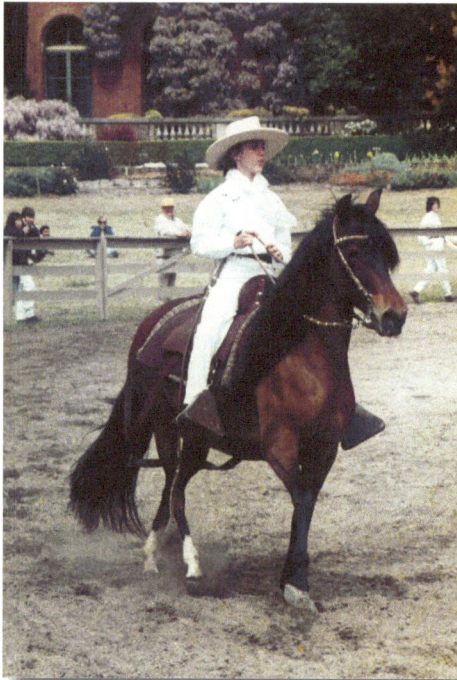

Lily and Rosie at
Filoli, a beautiful
estate in Woodside,
California

Lily and Rosie at the
La Bahia Show in
Watsonville,
California.
Lily and Rosie won
High Point Junior,
Age 12 and Under!

Lily and Rosie are 12 and Under High Point winners; the boy in the back is the 13 and Over winner.

We didn't love Rosie because she won in horse shows. We loved her because she was so special. She was like a horse from a fairy tale, but real.

Except for the night she had Tecolote, she was the sweetest, kindest, happiest horse.

But then she got sick … and died. Now she doesn't hurt anymore. She's in horse heaven, we think, with all the other good horses.

Rosie went to live with all the good horses.

Another Problem

Even though Rosie didn't hurt any more, we had another problem: Tecolote was alone. He had his friend, Shambho, and Shambho's mother, Avispa. But it wasn't the same as his own mom. And he didn't have a special grown-up horse to watch out for him. A special grown-up horse to make sure that he grew up to be a big horse with good manners who knew how to behave. What was Tecolote to do?

Tecolote was lonely.

Well, one thing about life—it doesn't stand still. Just when you think it's the end, something happens. It was time to separate Shambho from his mom.

After about five months, the mother horse doesn't make as much milk. And the milk she makes doesn't have as many vitamins and things in it to make the baby grow. Nature knows that it's time for that baby to grow up and eat hay like the big horses.

We put Shambho's mother with the other mares, and Teco and Shambho together in their own pasture.

Those colts were wild boys!

They had some rough and tumble days. They played and played, running and wrestling. *Especially Shambho!* Tecolote liked people and had good manners. But Shambho? No way. He was a wild child!

When Teco and Shambho lived together, we could catch Teco and give him medicine. We could trim his hooves if they grew too long. We could lead him from one place to another.

BUT NOT SHAMBHO! If he got hurt, we wouldn't be able to catch him and take care of him. Shambho had a mind of his own.

School

What were we going to do? Well, Tony knew the answer: The boys had to go to school. How do baby horses go to school?

They come out of their big pasture where they can run around and go into stalls. We moved them to a barn, just like big horses. They wore halters so we could catch them. Every day they had lessons, just like kids in school. Nothing too hard, just a little bit to learn every day.

The baby horses had to learn many things: how to let a person lead them, let someone touch them all over, and groom them. They had to learn to stand

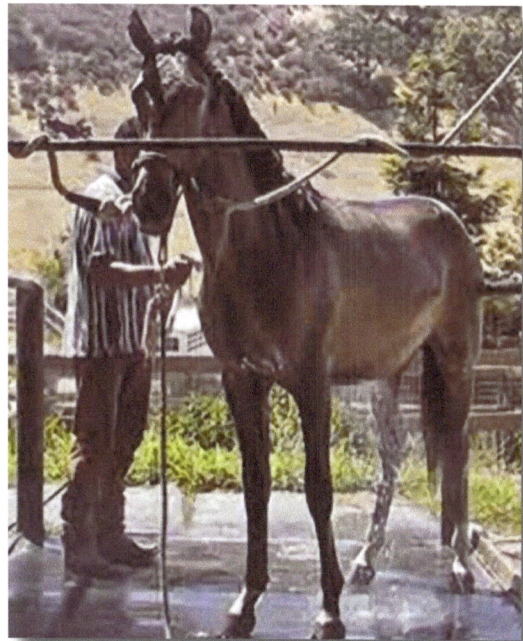

Tecolote's first bath

still so the vet could listen to their hearts and take care of them. The colts needed to learn to have their hooves picked up and trimmed if they grew too long.

Teco finished with his first lessons really fast. While Shambho was still learning, Teco was ready to go back to the pasture, but Shambho had to stay in his stall, learning how to be a good young horse.

We had a new problem: If we put Teco in a pasture by himself, he would be alone again. What should we do?

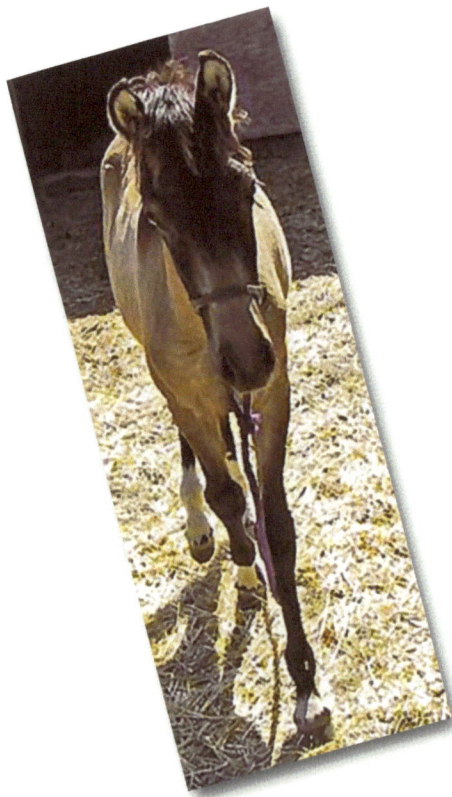

Tio Eddie

Well, something else happened at Rancho Vilasa—I got my bad knee fixed. I had a knee that hurt really a lot. I used to ride like this:

But my knee hurt too bad to do that anymore. I had to have my knee fixed and couldn't ride for a long time. My favorite horse, Eddie, was a big, strong horse. He had lots of energy and liked to be ridden and exercised very much. Sometimes, he ran around for fun.

Eddie liked to run.

When I couldn't ride him, Eddie became sad. He didn't run anymore. He stood with his head down. Sometimes he bullied the other horses in his pasture. He is a boss horse, and if he's not happy, he kicks and bites his friends. (Some people are like that, too. Do you know anyone like that?)

We had to put him in a pasture by himself so he wouldn't hurt the other horses. He became bored and lonely. One day he'd look in one direction; and the next day, the other.

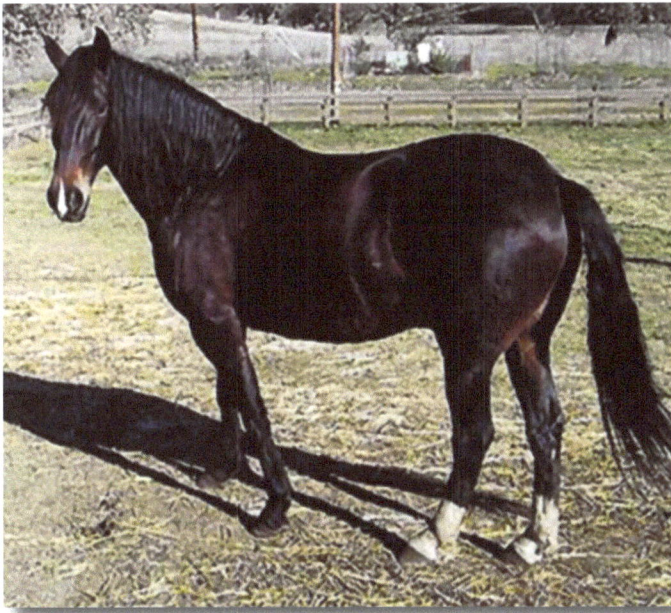

Eddie needed a job to do.

We asked ourselves, "Would a big horse like a little boy horse? Would a big horse that could be mean to big horses like a little boy horse?"

Hmm. We thought and thought.

Early one morning, we went out to the pasture. We put a halter on Eddie so we could catch him easily. We put a halter on Teco, so we could catch him, too.

We put them together in the pasture and stood by the gate so we could break up the fight if Eddie didn't like Tecolote.

What happened? Did Eddie chase Teco? Kick him? Bite him? What happened?

Eddie loved Teco! Now Teco had a big horse to love him and take care of him and see that he grew up right.

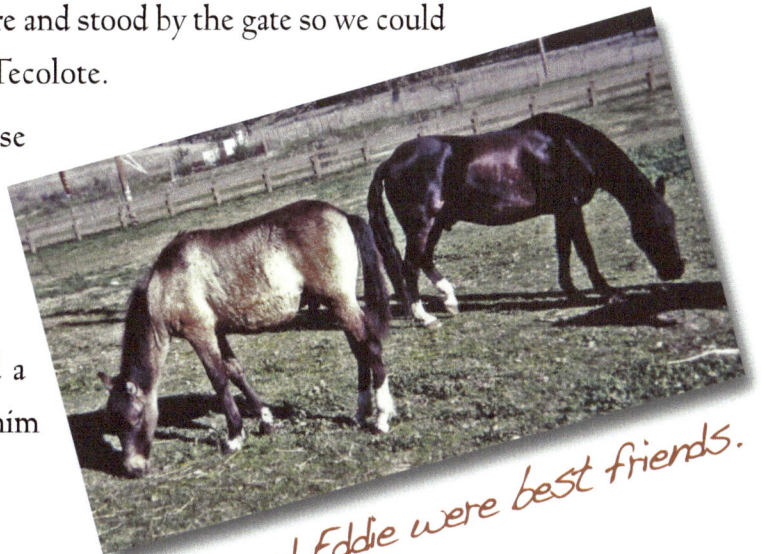

Teco and Eddie were best friends.

We started calling Eddie "Tio Eddie." "Tio" means "uncle" in Spanish. And that's how Eddie acted. He guarded Tecolote all the time.

If Teco was by the fence next to the road and Barry rode up on another horse, Eddie would come galloping over and put his ears back.

"Who are you? Stay away from my Tecolote!" he would say to the other horse. But once he recognized Barry's horse, he'd say, "Oh. I know you. You're okay. You can talk to Teco."

Really, Eddie said that. You just have to know how to speak "horse." They lived very happily in their pasture.

Eddie taught Teco to mind him. "I'm the boss, Tecolote. If you do what I say, I'll take care of you. I'll teach you how to be a big horse." And that's what Eddie did.

Everything was wonderful, except for one thing....

Shambho Needs a Friend

Another little boy horse lived on our ranch—Shambho. He finished his lessons, learning all he needed to know for a colt his age. He just took a little longer than Teco.

That doesn't mean that he wasn't smart. He just was a little more nervous and excitable, and took a little more handling to learn. Just like some children take a little longer to learn, Shambho took a bit more time. He was a good, smart boy and wanted to please.

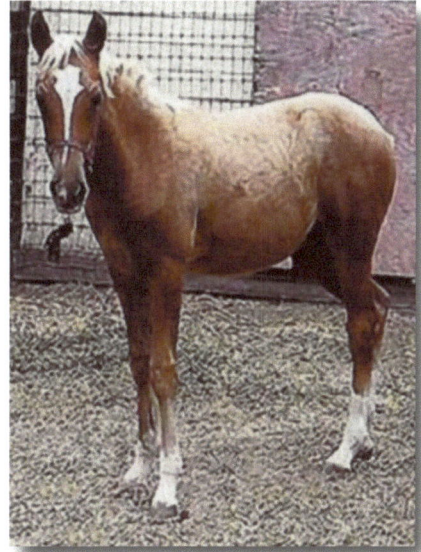

Shambho finished his lessons.

But where was he going to go? He couldn't stay by himself. He would get too lonely. Barry and Tony thought of Corcovado. Corcovado was a show horse.

Would Corco like little Shambho?

NO! When we put them together, Corco chased Shambho and bit him and kicked at him. Tony and Barry ran and got poor Shambho out of there fast.

Well, maybe Uncle Eddie would like Shambho. He already liked Tecolote. They put Shambho in with Eddie and Teco. Did Eddie like Shambho the way he did Teco?

Corcovado in a show

NO WAY! He chased him and bit him and tried to kick him, just like Corco did. I don't have any pictures of this because when it happened, everyone was running and running, trying to catch Shambho and keep Eddie away from him—and trying to keep safe themselves. People have to be very careful around horses. Even a baby horse can hurt you. Horses are very big and strong. If they run into you, it will hurt even if they don't mean to hurt you.

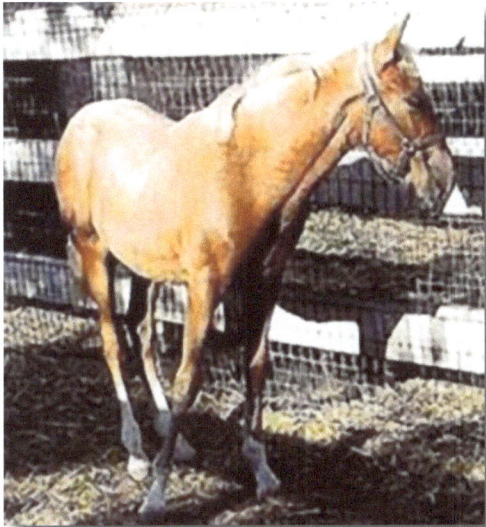

Poor Shambho was all alone.

Would Shambho have to live all alone his whole life? Would he never get to play with his buddy, Tecolote, the way they once did?

Barry realized what was wrong. The reason Eddie didn't like Shambho is: "The two horses had not been properly introduced!"

Don't you feel better when your mommy says, "Cara, this is my friend, Sally. Jarrett, this is my friend, Gregg. Would you like to play with them? Can they come to our house?"

Isn't it nicer to know someone before they come in your room and start playing with your favorite things?

That's how Eddie felt. He and Teco were very happy in their pasture, and all of a sudden this stranger showed up and wanted to play.

Shambho and Eddie lived next to each other in the barn.

Barry put Eddie and Shambho in stalls right next to each other. That way, they could talk over the fence.

"My name is Shambho. How do you do?"

"My name is Eddie. I'm fine."

And they could work out the rules:

"I'm a big horse, and you have to do what I want," Eddie said.

"Okay," Shambho said in horse talk. "I'll do what you want. Please don't hurt me and let me play with Tecolote."

"Okay. It's a deal."

What happened when they put them all together in the pasture?

They got along just fine. Uncle Eddie watched both boys and made sure they grew up to be well-mannered horses. The two boys got a big, special friend, and they all played with each other.

Our story is done for now. But is it over? No. Just like kids grow and change, so do baby horses. Kids go to nursery school and then they go to kindergarten. Next, elementary school. Then high school. Finally, college and, maybe, graduate school.

Teco, Shambho and Eddie became best friends.

Best friends

In a few months, Teco and Shambho will learn new lessons—a little at a time, slowly, not too much, nothing too scary. Then one day, we will be able to ride them.

Maybe you will ride Tecolote one day. But right now, it's time for them to be kids and live a happy life in the pasture with their Uncle Eddie.

So long, my friends. I hope you're growing up good and strong, protected by big people who love you—good grown-ups who will see that you become what you're meant to be when you're grown.

Goodbye for now.

When you grow up straight and tall, you'll teach your children to be like you, and they will teach theirs … and the world will become a beautiful place, smiling under the sun.

Tecolote grew up!
Barry and Tecolote love to go for rides.

THE END

About the author:

A lifelong horsewoman and award-winning author, Sandy Nathan is passionate about writing and horses. Her work reflects the many facets of her life––ranching, family life, and spiritual practice. She lives with her husband on her family's ranch and has three grown children and two grandchildren. "Tecolote reminds me of myself when I was a kid. In elementary school I was so shy that I didn't talk very much. I wanted to fit into my world as much as Tecolote wanted to fit into his. Tecolote shows us that stories with hard beginnings can have happy endings."

About the illustrations:

The illustrations in this book are snapshots that we took while Tecolote's story was happening. In using snapshots, we wanted to bring you as close to the action as possible and introduce you to the real Tecolote, Shambho, Rosie, and all the other horses of Rancho Vilasa. This truly is Tecolote's scrapbook—welcome to his world.

www.ingramcontent.com/pod-product-compliance
Lightning Source LLC
LaVergne TN
LVHW072108070426
835509LV00002B/69